DON'T PANIC
SATS

AUTUMN PUBLISHING

DON'T PANIC
SATS

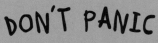

AUTUMN
PUBLISHING

Published in 2020
by Autumn Publishing
Cottage Farm
Sywell
NN6 0BJ
www.autumnpublishing.co.uk

Copyright © 2019 Autumn Publishing
Autumn is an imprint of Bonnier Books UK

0120 001
2 4 6 8 10 9 7 5 3 1
ISBN 978-1-83903-145-8

Written by Amy Italiano
Illustrated by Katie Abey

Designed by Chris Stanley
Edited by Suzanne Fossey

Printed and manufactured in China

An introduction

In Key Stage 2 SATs, you will complete three English test papers.

The first test is a Grammar and Punctuation test. You will have 45 minutes to complete it. The first set of pages in this book (pp.4–24) cover topics you will need for the grammar questions. The next set of pages (pp.26–32) look at punctuation that you may be asked about.

Next, you will be given a short Spelling test. There will be 20 words that you will be asked to spell to complete pre-written sentences. This test isn't timed but will take around 15 minutes. Pages 34–36 in this book focus on spelling.

Lastly, you will complete a Reading paper. You will be asked to read three texts and answer questions about them. This will last for 1 hour. Pages 38–42 of this book will help you to answer these questions.

Parent Guide

Each topic has a guide with tips that you can use to help your child understand and become confident with each subject.

Contents

Nouns and Adjectives

Nouns

A **noun** is a word for a person, place or thing. There are different types of noun. A **common noun** is a general word which describes everyday objects, e.g. table, man, country. A **proper noun** requires a capital letter because it is a particular name given to a person, place or thing, e.g. Tom, London, America.

Put a circle around the common nouns and a rectangle around the proper nouns in the box below:

①
run	big	England	clever
jump	plant	bucket	Jennifer
classroom	Mrs Smith	gnome	quickly

Pronouns

A pronoun can be used to replace a noun to avoid repetition.

For example: **The man** was asleep because **the man** had been working hard.
The man was asleep because **he** had been working hard.

Using "the man" twice sounds strange, so we can replace the second noun with a pronoun: "he".

Instead of repeating the noun in these sentences, use a pronoun:

② "Can you take your coat off and hang [ ] on your peg?"

③ The woman fixed the car and then [ ] packed her tools away.

④ David and I bought ice-creams and shared them with [ ] friends.

Parent Guide

Try to think of exciting adjectives to describe things that you and your child talk about. Challenge one another to collect high quality vocabulary from texts that you read and use these adjectives whenever you can.

Adjectives

Adjectives are words that describe nouns. Usually, they go before the noun but can sometimes be near the noun elsewhere in the sentence.

Write a suitable adjective to describe these nouns:

⑤ the [ ] cake

⑥ the boy was [ ]

⑦ a [ ] apple

⑧ the hole is [ ]

4

Practice Questions

(1) What word class is <u>his</u> in this sentence?

Jack threw his ball too far and it landed over the fence.

Tick one

A common noun ☐

A proper noun ☐

A pronoun ☐

An adjective ☐

1 mark

(2) Circle three **adjectives** in this sentence.

The sunset was magnificent. It created a red and orange haze across the sky.

1 mark

(3) Circle three **nouns** in this sentence.

Amelie hugged her teddy and was filled with happiness.

1 mark

(4) Circle each **lower case letter** that should be a **capital letter.**

laura couldn't wait to arrive in edinburgh to meet her cousin john on tuesday.

1 mark

(5) Which sentence uses the underlined word as a **noun?**

Tick one

I was excited to <u>fly</u> on an aeroplane for my holiday. ☐

The light was <u>fluorescent</u> and bright. ☐

George swatted at the <u>fly</u> wearily. ☐

It is fun to <u>flick</u> paper into the bin. ☐

1 mark

(6) Choose an appropriate **noun** for this sentence.

Aunt Mabel couldn't contain her

_____ when she saw

her new car.

1 mark

(7) Choose the correct pair of **pronouns** to complete this sentence.

_____ couldn't find the ball and had to ask someone to help _____ .

Tick one

Him   them   ☐

She   her   ☐

She   his   ☐

They   our   ☐

1 mark

(8) Add a suffix to make this word an **adjective**.

friend_____

1 mark

Answers on page 44

Verbs and Adverbs

Verbs

A verb is a "**doing**" **word** — it tells us about what someone has, is or does.

For example: *Amir **ran** all the way to his friend's house. He didn't **stop**.*
*I **am** 11 years old. I **have** 16 fish.*

Underline the verbs in these sentences:

① I was exhausted, so I slept until midday.

② My teacher thought the classroom was too noisy, so she told everyone to be quiet.

Adverbs

Adverbs give you more information about a verb. They might describe **how, when or where** something happened. Adverbs often end with "-ly", which makes them easy to spot, e.g. "The girl skipped **happily**". Don't be tricked, though; sometimes they don't end in "-ly".

Use suitable adverbs from the box to complete these sentences:

③ Simon _____ replaces the lid of the vase.

④ The builder _____ whistled a tune while he worked.

⑤ _____, I ran to the door and knocked on it _____.

| merrily |
| twice |
| carefully |
| quickly |

Modal Verbs

Modal verbs are used to describe **possibility,** or how likely something is, e.g. **could**, **might**.

Underline the modal verbs in the sentences below:

⑥ You should take your shoes off before stepping on the carpet.

⑦ The boy thought that he might win first prize.

Parent Guide

Play a miming game such as charades, where players guess the action being demonstrated to help reinforce verbs as "doing" words. Children often fall into the trap of looking for "-ly" words when seeking adverbs. Remind them that this is not always the case!

Answers on page 44

Practice Questions

① Circle four **verbs** in these sentences.

The optician was very professional when she tested my eyes. She recommended that I wear my glasses.

1 mark

② What is the **word class** of the underlined words?

a. I sang the song underlined{enthusiastically}.

b. Her speech was very underlined{enthusiastic}.

1 mark

③ Explain how the **modal verb** changes the meaning of the second sentence.

We will go to the cinema after this job is complete.

We might go to the cinema after this job is complete.

_____

_____

_____

1 mark

④ In which sentence is the **adverb** underlined?

Tick one

I hastily unwrapped the present. ☐

The wrapping paper was lovely. ☐

Sally had given me the present. ☐

She was a friendly girl. ☐

1 mark

⑤ Which ending would turn the word happy into an **adverb**?

Tick one

happi**est** ☐
happi**ness** ☐
happi**er** ☐
happi**ly** ☐

1 mark

⑥ Circle the **adverb** in this sentence.

Sindy arrived at her audition early.

1 mark

⑦ Underline the **modal verb** in this sentence.

Archie hoped that he would play tennis again.

1 mark

⑧ Which word shows **what** Sarah did?

Tick one

Sarah laughed so loud that everyone could hear.

↑ ☐   ↑ ☐   ↑ ☐   ↑ ☐

1 mark

Answers on page 44

Determiners and Prepositions

Determiners

A **determiner** is a word that comes *before* a noun to describe how many or which noun is being discussed. For example:

a big bird	*the* red post-box
both legs	*three* happy children

The words "**a**", "**an**" and "**the**" are special types of determiners called **articles**.

Circle four articles and underline three other determiners in these sentences:

① On the beach, I saw many stones, some pebbles and two starfish.

② A log had washed onto the sand, where an insect landed on it.

Prepositions

Prepositions are words which describe time, place or cause, e.g. **when, where** or **why** something happened. For example, a cat might jump *on* a chair or *over* a chair – the preposition tells us **where** it jumped. You might sing a song *before* or *after* brushing your teeth – the preposition tells us **when** you did it.

Use the prepositions in the box to complete the following sentences:

③ The man fell asleep [_____] the show even though the acrobat was

climbing [_____] the rope ladder to the most amazing heights!

④ Harry wiggled [_____] the tunnel [_____] cartwheeling

across the garden.

⑤ My dog hid [_____] my dad's suitcase that had been left

[_____] the front door.

through
behind
up
during
by
before

Parent Guide

Look for ways to remember certain things about each word class. A **determiner** can **determine** how many of an item there are and a **preposition** can tell you about an object's **position**.

Practice Questions

① Circle three **determiners** in this sentence.

I asked Jane to lend me a pencil but she didn't have any spare ones. I borrowed the teacher's pen instead.

1 mark

② Underline three **prepositions** in these sentences.

During the cricket match, I saw one ball hit a spectator on the head and another roll under the hot dog stand.

1 mark

③ Which **word class** is underlined in this sentence?

The show on TV went on for <u>an</u> extraordinary length of time.

Tick one

Adverb ☐
Article ☐
Adjective ☐
Preposition ☐

1 mark

④ Match the **determiners** to the correct **nouns**.

a   bananas

some   octopus

an   tambourine

1 mark

⑤ Complete this sentence, using suitable **prepositions**.

My dog ran _____ my garden and then squeezed _____ the fence.

1 mark

⑥ Add a suitable **article** to this sentence.

Jenny picked up _____ orange.

1 mark

⑦ Sort the words into the correct columns.

under	every	those	on
between	after	the	an

Determiners	Prepositions

1 mark

⑧ Correct the **article** that has been used incorrectly in this sentence.

My dad decided to cook dinner, so he went to the shop and bought a right ingredients for the recipe.

1 mark

Synonyms and Antonyms

Synonyms

Synonyms are words which have the same or similar meaning to one another, e.g. "big" and "large", or "happy" and "cheerful".

Match up the words that are synonyms:

① **a.** Quick

Tired

b. Amiable

Rare

c. Sleepy

Rapid

d. Tall

Eccentric

e. Unusual

Friendly

f. Mad

Towering

Antonyms

Antonyms are words which have an opposite meaning to one another, e.g. "hot" and "cold", or "modern" and "old-fashioned".

Write an antonym for each of these words:

② Delicious

③ Frightening

④ Ancient

⑤ Silly

⑥ Cry

⑦ Strong

⑧ Excited

⑨ Fascinating

Parent Guide

Children learn and can name basic opposites from a young age. It is important to continue discussing words and increasing their vocabulary through reading. High-quality books will develop their understanding of the meaning of more complex words. This development can have a powerful effect on their writing, too.

Answers on page 44

Practice Questions

① Which of these words is an **antonym** of <u>important</u>?

We were missing an <u>important</u> piece of information to solve the puzzle.

Tick one

Vital ☐

Crucial ☐

Insignificant ☐

Colourful ☐

1 mark

② Underline two words in these sentences below which are **synonyms**.

The pirate had captured many prisoners on his wild voyages. After they had been trapped and tickled mercilessly, they were made to walk the plank.

1 mark

③ Which adjective is a **synonym** of the word <u>unceasing</u>?

Tick one

Careless ☐

Endless ☐

Heartless ☐

Pointless ☐

1 mark

④ Write an **antonym** which could replace the underlined word in this sentence.

At the museum, Samira was stunned by the paintings and thought that they were <u>beautiful</u>.

Antonym: ☐

1 mark

⑤ Are these two words **synonyms** or **antonyms**?

Lethargic   Energetic

☐

1 mark

⑥ Write four **antonyms** of the word <u>nice</u>.

☐ ☐

☐ ☐

1 mark

⑦ Match up these **synonyms**.

a. Precisely   Devoted

b. Joyful   Authentic

c. Real   Exactly

d. Loyal   Happy

1 mark

⑧ Change the words to **antonyms** to alter the meaning of this sentence.

It was a very hot day and I felt

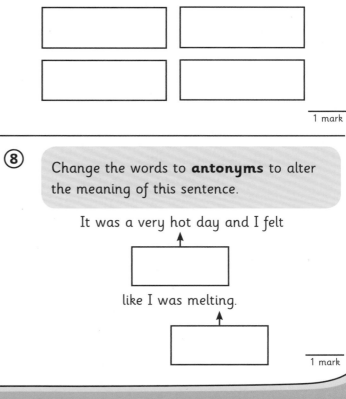

like I was melting.

1 mark

Answers on page 44

Subject and Object

Subject

The **subject** of a sentence is the person or thing who is doing the action that is described. This person or thing is usually named just before the verb, and they are often the main focus of the sentence. In the following sentence, Johnny is the subject and he is named just before the verb: "finished".

For example: *Yesterday,* **Johnny** *finished the book.*

Circle the subjects in these sentences:

① The bird landed on the table and pecked at the seeds.

② My fireworks shot thunderously into the air.

③ Before leaving the station, the man bought a return ticket.

④ Sarah had forgotten to bring her packed lunch to school today.

Object

A sentence might have only a subject and a verb, e.g. **Tom jumped**. But it may also contain an **object** which is acted upon by the verb, e.g. **Tom jumped onto the chair**. The "chair" is the object that Tom jumped onto. The object often follows the verb.

Choose a sensible object from the box to complete these sentences:

⑤ I washed my .... with warm water.

⑥ Well done, you have passed the .... !

⑦ The cup landed on the .... and smashed.

⑧ My hair was knotty because I couldn't find my ....

| floor |
| telephone |
| quickly |
| test |
| English |
| jump |
| hair |
| brush |

Parent Guide
The difference between subjects and objects is the action expressed by the verb, e.g. "Tom studies English" – Tom is the subject and English is the object. Think of different sentences and ask your child to work out the subjects and objects in each one.

Practice Questions

① Write **subject** or **object** below each underlined word.

The <u>plumber</u> discovered a leaking <u>pipe</u>

a. [↑]   **b.** [↑]

so <u>he</u> mended the <u>hole</u> quickly.

c. [↑]   **d.** [↑]

1 mark

② Label the word in bold as the **subject** or **object** in these sentences.

a. I wrote the **letter** hastily.

b. The **box** smelt of chips.

c. **Gill** impatiently waited for the bus.

d. I couldn't believe my **eyes**!

1 mark

③ Circle the **subject** in this sentence.

The tree bent forlornly in the howling wind.

1 mark

④ Circle two **subjects** and underline two **objects** in this sentence.

Wearily, the children climbed the stairs; they had been playing football for hours.

1 mark

⑤ Write **S** (subject) and **O** (object) in the correct boxes.

Jim opened the present excitedly.

a. [↑]   **b.** [↑]

1 mark

⑥ Underline the correct **pronouns** in this sentence.

My sister absolutely loves roller-coasters.

She/Her is always watching films about

they/them.

1 mark

⑦ Label the word in bold as the **subject** or **object** in these sentences.

a. Very slowly, **Pandora** opened the box.

b. Very slowly, Pandora opened the **box**.

1 mark

⑧ Write **V** (verb), **S** (subject), **A** (adjective) and **O** (object) and in the correct boxes.

We counted our chocolate coins.

a. [↑]   **b.** [↑]   **c.** [↑]   **d.** [↑]

1 mark

Clauses

Main Clause

A **clause** is a group of words that contain a subject and a verb. A **main clause** is the part of a sentence that makes sense on its own. If other words around the main clause are removed, it will still stand as a complete sentence. In the example below, "Jim cleaned the windows" is the main clause. It has a subject (Jim) and a verb (cleaned), and it makes sense on its own.

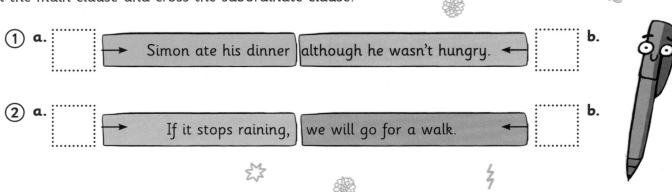

Because it was a sunny day, ***Jim cleaned the windows.***

Subordinate Clause

A **subordinate clause** is an extra piece of information which does not make sense on its own. In the example above, "Because it was a sunny day" does not make sense on its own. This is a subordinate clause.

Tick the main clause and cross the subordinate clause:

① a. [ ] → | Simon ate his dinner | although he wasn't hungry. | ← [ ] b.

② a. [ ] → | If it stops raining, | we will go for a walk. | ← [ ] b.

Relative Clause

A **relative clause** is a type of subordinate clause which gives information about a noun using words such as **which**, **who**, **whose** or **that**.

For example:

The goalkeeper, ***who is 9 years old****, made a fantastic save.*

Underline the relative clauses in the following sentences:

③ I baked a cake that was delicious.

④ Jim beckoned the boy whose ball had bounced over the fence.

⑤ I liked the bedroom that had bunk beds inside.

⑥ The cat, who is now hiding under the car, has scratched our sofa.

> ### Parent Guide
> Encourage your child to say each part of the sentence aloud to identify whether it is a main or subordinate clause. Saying "because it was a sunny day..." aloud should help them to realise that it is incomplete and doesn't make sense without an adjoining main clause.

Practice Questions

① Name the type of **clause** underlined in this sentence.

Mandy put her coat on <u>even though it wasn't raining.</u>

[ ] 1 mark

② Write a **relative clause** to complete this sentence.

I picked up the orange, _____

_____, and

threw it in the bin.

1 mark

③ What type of clause is underlined in this sentence?

If you tickle me any more, <u>I will scream</u>.

[ ] 1 mark

④ Underline the relative clause in each of these sentences.

a. I chose a book that looked appealing.

b. The clown whose nose fell off was hilarious.

1 mark

⑤ Identify each underlined **clause** by ticking the correct column.

		Main Clause	Subordinate Clause
a.	Nadia jumped up <u>as soon as she heard the doorbell.</u>		
b.	<u>While the customer looked at the menu,</u> the waiter sighed.		
c.	<u>I've made a cake</u> so that you can have a slice.		
d.	Once you've finished your dinner, <u>we can go for a walk.</u>		

1 mark

⑥ Underline the **subordinate clause** in this sentence.

While Bailey slept on the sofa, Sam gnawed

on the leg of the table.

1 mark

⑦ Underline the **subordinate clause** in this sentence.

Steve gasped because he had always

wanted a cat.

1 mark

Phrases

Noun Phrases

A **phrase** is a group of words or small part of a sentence. The words in the phrase will make sense together, e.g. "a green box", but will not make a complete sentence because they do not contain a verb.

A **noun phrase** is a group of words built around a noun which gives more information about that noun. For example, "umbrella" is a noun, and "the holey umbrella" is a noun phrase.

Underline the noun phrases in these sentences:

① My mum had bought me a new watch.

② The rickety roller-coaster trundled around the track.

③ The boy with the stripy trainers fell over.

④ The purple house is for sale.

Adverbials

Can you remember what an adverb is? *(If you can't, look back at page 6.)* That's right, an adverb gives us more information about a verb. An **adverbial** works in the same way: it is a word, group of words or phrase which gives us more information about the verb in the sentence. It might tell us **how, where** or **when** something happened.

For example: *I played football **last night.***   (*when* I played)

*We chatted **under the bridge**.* (*where* we chatted)

Fronted adverbials can be used as interesting openers to your sentences. These are adverbials that sit at the beginning of a sentence. They are often followed by a comma.

Can you move the **adverbials in bold** from the examples above to the front of each sentence?

⑤ [..] I played football.

⑥ [..] we chatted.

Now add your own fronted adverbial to the start of this sentence:

⑦ [..] she stood and waited.

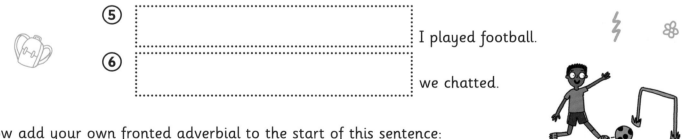

Answers on page 45

Practice Questions

1 What is the **grammatical** name for the underlined part of this sentence?

The radiant sunshine filled the sky.

[   ]

1 mark

2 Circle the **adverbial** in this sentence.

Last Tuesday, I broke my arm.

1 mark

3 Underline the **noun phrase** in this sentence.

I jumped from the tall, strong tree with thick branches.

1 mark

4 What is the **grammatical name** for the underlined part of this sentence?

All night long, I tossed and turned in bed.

[   ]

1 mark

5 Rewrite this sentence so that it begins with the **adverbial**.

John painted the fence after dinner.

_____

_____

1 mark

6 Rewrite this sentence so that it ends with the **adverbial**.

In an instant, the magician had disappeared.

_____

_____

1 mark

7 Write an interesting **noun phrase** using the noun wardrobe.

_____

_____

_____

1 mark

Parent Guide

Helping your child to remember the key points about different types of clauses and phrases will be most helpful:
Relative clause: relates using "who", "which", etc.
Noun phrase: information about a noun.

Conjunctions

Coordinating Conjunctions

A **conjunction** is a word that is used to connect two parts of a sentence.
Coordinating conjunctions connect two parts of a sentence that are of equal importance.

For example: *I might go for a bike ride **or** I might read a book.*

There are 7 coordinating conjunctions which can be remembered by the acronym FANBOYS:

F A N B O Y S

for   and   nor   but   or   yet   so

Use a coordinating conjunction to complete this sentence:

 ① Yolanda liked apples ⬚⬚⬚⬚⬚ Joshua didn't.

Subordinating Conjunctions

A **subordinating conjunction** introduces a subordinate clause. It creates a part of a sentence which doesn't make sense by itself. Remember that a sentence can begin with a subordinate clause, so a subordinating conjunction may be at the start of a sentence!

For example:

> *Yolanda liked apples **if** they were fresh and crunchy.*
>
> ***Because** he didn't like apples, Joshua ate a banana.*

Circle the subordinating conjunctions in these sentences:

② Although I'd love to, I can't make it to your party.

③ Fry the chicken until it has browned.

④ If you don't hurry up, we'll be late.

⑤ He was annoyed because the train had stopped.

⑥ I'm staying in today so that I don't miss the postman.

Parent Guide

Children often forget that subordinating conjunctions can begin sentences. Plenty of practice moving clauses around in a sentence (e.g. "I ate quickly so that I could play outside" or "So that I could play outside, I ate quickly") will help to remind them to check the start as well as the middle of the sentence for conjunctions.

Answers on page 45

Practice Questions

① Identify the word class of the underlined word in this sentence.

The crocodile loved to swim <u>so</u> he walked to the river each morning.

	Tick one
An adverb	☐
A coordinating conjunction	☐
A subordinating conjunction	☐
A determiner	☐

1 mark

② Explain how the conjunctions in these two sentences change their meaning.

After you eat your apple, we'll play a game.

If you eat your apple, we'll play a game.

_____

_____

_____ 1 mark

③ Circle the coordinating conjunction in this sentence.

Wherever we go on holiday, I will be

careful neither to sunbathe nor to go

out without wearing sun cream.

1 mark

④ Write a subordinating conjunction to complete this sentence.

_____ you eat your

lunch, you must wash your hands.

1 mark

⑤ Complete the subordinating conjunction that begins this sentence.

Even _____ it was night

time, the street was very busy.

1 mark

⑥ Circle the coordinating conjunction in this sentence.

While Noel was looking the other way,

Matthew ran and hid behind the tree.

1 mark

⑦ Underline the coordinating conjunctions in these sentences.

It was really sunny outside and I knew that the swings at the park would be empty. I told my dad that

I didn't want to go to school but he said that I had to because he was going to work, so there would be

no-one to look after me.

1 mark

Answers on page 45

Tenses

> I flew into space in a rocket!

> I am flying into space in a rocket!

> I will fly into space in a rocket!

What is the difference between these three sentences? That's right, they have been written in different tenses, which is shown by the changing verb.

> The first one is written in the **past tense.** It shows that you have already been to space by using the verb "flew".

> The second one is written in the **present tense**. It shows that you are currently flying into space by using the verb "fly".

> The last sentence is written to describe a **future time**. It uses the word "will" to show that you are going into space at a later date.

Rewrite the sentence "I throw a ball to my friend, Jack" in both **past tense** and **future time**:

① **Past tense:**

② **Future time:**

Present Progressive

The **present progressive** tense shows that the verb is happening *right now*, using the words "is", "am" and "are", and adding "-ing" to the verb.

Write "is", "am" and "are", and add "-ing" to write these sentences in the present progressive:

③ I .... paint .... a picture.

④ He .... kick .... a football.

⑤ They .... walk .... around the lake.

Parent Guide

Look out for irregular verbs that don't have "-ed" added to them to create the past tense and discuss these with your child, e.g. "buy" and "bought", or "blow" and "blew". Trying them with "-ed" (e.g. "buyed" and "blowed") can sound humorous and help your child to "hear" correct grammar.

Answers on page 46

Practice Questions

1 Which sentence is grammatically correct?

Tick one

I reached up and take the toy down. ☐

I reach up and will take the toy down. ☐

I reached up and took the toy down. ☐

I will reach up and took the toy down ☐

1 mark

2 Rewrite the sentence in the **past tense**, changing the underlined verbs.

Sally <u>bakes</u> cookies and <u>eats</u> them within five days.

_____

_____

_____

1 mark

3 Tick the sentence that is **closest in meaning** to the statement.

I was enjoying an adventure book the other day.

Tick one

I will enjoy an adventure book tomorrow. ☐

I will be enjoying an adventure book soon. ☐

I am enjoying an adventure book right now. ☐

I enjoyed an adventure book recently. ☐

1 mark

4 Rewrite this sentence so that it is in the **present progressive tense.**

I watched an amazing film.

_____

_____

_____

1 mark

5 Change the verbs in this sentence so that it is written in the **present tense**.

I was eight years old and I had my own rabbit.

_____

_____

_____

1 mark

6 Write the **past tense** of the following verbs.

buy	
ride	
sleep	
worry	
find	

1 mark

Active and Passive Voice

Active Voice

If a sentence is written in the **active** voice, the subject is doing the verb. They are being **active**!

Underline the subject in these active voice sentences:

① The man walked across the field.

② The candle shone brightly.

③ Stewart drank a large glass of water hurriedly.

④ I ran the obstacle course in record time.

⑤ We are going to watch a movie tonight.

Passive Voice

If the subject has something done to them, then they are said to be **passive**. The subject is *not* doing the verb. A sentence written like this is in the **passive voice**.

Underline the subject in these passive voice sentences:

⑥ The man was tripped up by the log.

⑦ The candle was blown out by the wind.

⑧ Stewart has been soaked.

⑨ The obstacle course was run by lots of people.

⑩ The movie is going to be shown to us tonight.

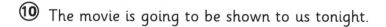

Parent Guide

Help your child to find the subject and verb in a sentence and discuss it together. Is the subject doing the verb? Or is the subject being acted upon by the verb? This is a tricky concept and may need a lot of practice.

Practice Questions

① Decide whether these sentences use **active** or **passive voice** and put a tick in the correct column.

		Active Voice	Passive Voice
a.	I screwed up the piece of paper.		
b.	The car was towed by the truck.		
c.	All of the plates had been smashed.		
d.	The lightning struck the tree.		
e.	The science class viewed the comet.		
f.	The savannah is roamed by beautiful giraffes.		
g.	The novel was read by Mum in one day.		
h.	The kangaroo carried her baby in her pouch.		

1 mark

② Rewrite this sentence, changing it into the **active voice**.

The lettuce was eaten by the rabbit.

_____

_____

_____

_____

1 mark

③ Rewrite this sentence, changing it into the **passive voice**.

Jacqueline baked the cake.

_____

_____

_____

_____

1 mark

④ Which of these sentences uses the **passive voice**?

Tick one

Annabelle organised a party. ☐

She bought all the food and drinks. ☐

The balloons were very kindly donated. ☐

The DJ was absolutely brilliant! ☐

1 mark

⑤ Write a sentence about a dog, using the **active voice.**

_____

_____

_____

_____

1 mark

Standard English

Standard English is the grammatically correct writing that you might find in newspapers or books. It has a formal sound and follows all the English grammar rules.

One of the important rules of Standard English is making sure that nouns and verbs agree. This is particularly important with pronouns and plurals.

For example:

He **was** going to the shops. My hand **is** dirty.

They **were** going to the shops. My hands **are** dirty.

Try these:

① I ⬚⬚⬚⬚ going to the shops.

② We ⬚⬚⬚⬚ going to the shops.

③ The window ⬚⬚⬚⬚ dirty.

④ The windows ⬚⬚⬚⬚ dirty.

Formal writing uses Standard English. You might write formally when writing to the Queen or inviting people to a wedding.

Formal writing does not use contractions, e.g. "isn't" or "shouldn't", and sounds calm, not overly excited. It uses appropriate vocabulary, not words or abbreviations that you would use when chatting to your friend, e.g. "ain't" or "hi".

Circle **four** parts of this note which show that it is not written formally:

⑤

> Hey bud! You up for going to the park later? It isn't supposed to be raining. Where'd be a good place to meet?

Parent Guide
Discuss with your child colloquialisms or slang that you hear people use. Point out nouns and verbs that don't agree and which parts should be changed to sound grammatically correct. Have fun together trying to talk in the most formal manner possible; how long can you keep it up?

Practice Questions

① Which sentence is the most **formal**?

Tick one

I didn't like the film. ☐

I hated the film! ☐

I did not enjoy the film. ☐

The film's awful! ☐

1 mark

② Circle the most formal word in each pair to complete this letter.

I wish to **complain / moan** about the terrible service I received this morning.

The food **wasn't / was not** cooked properly and the service was **poor / rubbish.**

I should **have/of** left immediately.

1 mark

③ Which sentence is written in **Standard English?**

Tick one

The birds was eating their food. ☐

I wish you'd drew me a picture. ☐

They were singing beautifully. ☐

He look at my house. ☐

1 mark

④ Which sentence is grammatically correct?

Tick one

Yesterday, I will oversleep. ☐

I can't wait to see a dolphin. ☐

I walked to the shop and see my friend. ☐

Next week they skipped home. ☐

1 mark

⑤ Circle the correct word so that each sentence is written in **Standard English.**

I **buyed/bought** myself a new dress.

We **did/done** very well in the competition.

Them/The rabbits really liked carrots.

1 mark

⑥ Rewrite this sentence so that it is written in **Standard English.**

That was the man what found my cat.

_____

_____

_____

1 mark

⑦ Which word completes the sentence in **Standard English?**

My dad .... me how to ride my bike.

Tick one

teached ☐

taught ☐

teach ☐

1 mark

⑧ Write the correct **past tense** of these verbs.

a. drive

b. kick

c. eat

d. drink

e. find

f. run

1 mark

Basic Punctuation

Well done for making your way through all of your Grammar work! Let's look at some basic ways to punctuate your sentences. This should be easy work for superstars like you!

Capital letters are used to start every sentence and proper noun:

The bird ate the apple in August.

Full stops are used the end of a normal sentence:

The apple had fallen from the tree.

Question marks are used at the end of a question:

Why did the tree lose its leaves?

Exclamation marks are used to create energy, e.g. when something is exciting or shocking:

The firework display was incredible!

Commas can be used to separate items in a list or to show a break in a sentence. Commas are often used when adverbials or subordinate clauses are at the beginning of a sentence:

I took biscuits, sweets, fruit and a sandwich.

Before turning off the light, I pulled the curtains.

Find **five** basic punctuation errors on this sign:

①

LOST DOG

Can you help. A black dog has gone missing from the area He was last seen yesterday morning. he has a white tail blue eyes and a red collar. Please knock at 7 King street if you find him

Practice Questions

① Which sentence should end with a **question mark**?

Tick one

I asked him if he liked the cake. ☐

She didn't know whether to go right or left. ☐

Are you going to bed early. ☐

I wonder why the sky is blue. ☐

1 mark

② Insert a **comma** into this sentence.

As fast as possible the

boy ran home.

1 mark

③ Which sentence should end with an **exclamation mark**?

Tick one

I had a delicious lunch. ☐

What an amazing show. ☐

What are you doing now. ☐

The stars were lovely. ☐

1 mark

④ Which sentence is punctuated correctly?

Tick one

Amazingly, he escaped without blood sweat or tears. ☐

Amazingly he escaped without blood, sweat or tears. ☐

Amazingly, he escaped without blood, sweat or tears. ☐

Amazingly he escaped without blood sweat or tears. ☐

1 mark

⑤ Complete these sentences by adding the correct punctuation.

a. Are you playing tomorrow

b. What a fantastic night

c. I am very tired

1 mark

⑥ Add the missing **full stops** to this paragraph.

We decided that we should meet at the park and play at three o'clock We jumped on our bikes and cycled as fast as we could towards the park I wanted to be the first one on the swings so I pedalled really, really fast I was like lightning!

1 mark

Parent Guide

Children often have good understanding of basic punctuation but struggle to apply it when editing their own writing. Encourage them to read aloud and take note of where they pause, stop, question or add emphasis. Have they used appropriate punctuation at these points?

More Punctuation

Here is some more complex punctuation that you may have started to use in your writing.

Colons can be used to introduce a list or a piece of information that explains what you have just said.

I gathered four ingredients for the cake: flour, sugar, butter and eggs.

Mary was exhausted: she had spent all day digging in the garden.

Semi-colons are used to link two clauses or sentences that are related to each other.

Jim told funny jokes; I laughed every time.

The storm in the night was very loud; I didn't sleep well.

Brackets, commas and dashes can be used to add extra pieces of information to a sentence. This extra piece of information is called parenthesis.

I returned the book (a science fiction classic) to the library yesterday.

The clouds, which were grey and stormy, hovered above us all day.

They caught many fish – trout and salmon – at the river on Sunday.

Hyphens are used to link two or more words to help a sentence make sense. They can be used with numbers, ages, names, prefixes and words that are related.

Mrs Hall-Dawson was a sixty-year-old woman who was not old-fashioned.

She had collected twenty-two pairs of shoes from every decade since the mid-1960s.

Choose whether these sentences need a colon or a semi-colon:

		Colon	Semi-colon
①	I need these ingredients salt, pasta, rice and mint.		
②	I'm going to watch a movie the reviews were good.		
③	I want to play outside I don't like being cooped up inside.		
④	I've been to four countries France, Spain, India and Norway.		

Parent Guide

Higher level punctuation covered on these pages may have been recently introduced to your child in school. Reading lots and becoming familiar with how and where punctuation is used effectively is the first step to internalising its use. This is vital to help children – and adults! – become confident at using it in their own writing.

Practice Questions

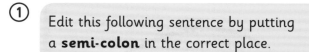 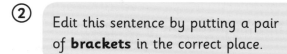

① Edit this following sentence by putting a **semi-colon** in the correct place.

My uncle was saving up to buy a new motorbike he said he would take me out on it.

1 mark

② Edit this sentence by putting a pair of **brackets** in the correct place.

It is Rachel's goal to climb many mountains such as Snowdon and Ben Nevis before she is 25.

1 mark

③ Which sentence has the correct punctuation?

Tick one

I am visiting the seaside my favourite place – next week!	
I am visiting – the seaside – my favourite place next week!	
I am visiting – the seaside my favourite place next week!	
I am visiting the seaside – my favourite place – next week!	

1 mark

④ Insert a **hyphen** to link two words in this sentence.

It is a well presented project.

1 mark

⑤ Insert a **colon** to punctuate this sentence.

Laura loved holidays for two reasons spending time with her family and getting lots of sleep!

1 mark

⑥ Add a pair of **commas** to this sentence.

The cat who had been watching the bird all morning finally pounced... and missed!

1 mark

Inverted Commas

Punctuating speech with inverted commas (or "speech marks") comes with lots of rules! Here are three top tips for punctuating conversations:

Put a capital letter at the start of the speech:

Hello said John.

Put a pair of inverted commas around the words that have been said:

"Hello" said John.

Separate the speech and the reporting clause with a comma (or a question mark or exclamation mark). Punctuation at the end of speech goes INSIDE the inverted commas:

"Hello," said John.

Now it's your turn to follow the steps!

① Put a capital letter at the start of the speech:

I replied _____onjour!

② Put a pair of inverted commas around the words that have been said:

I replied ____Bonjour!____

③ Separate the speech and the reporting clause with a comma:

I replied____ "Bonjour!"

④ See if you can apply all three steps by rewriting the next line:

are you having a good day asked John.

_____

_____

Parent Guide
There are lots of steps to follow when punctuating speech. Reading it aloud can help a child to hear which words are direct speech and should be enclosed with inverted commas. Prompt them to check for capital letters and other punctuation marks.

Practice Questions

① Which sentence has the correct punctuation?

Tick one

"which drink would you like?" asked the waiter.	☐
"Which drink would you like?" asked the waiter.	☐
"Which drink would you like," asked the waiter.	☐
"Which drink would you like"? asked the waiter.	☐

1 mark

---

② "Would you like to watch a film?" Sally asked Jo.

Jo tells Sally that she would love to. Write her response using **inverted commas** and the tips you have learnt.

_____

_____

1 mark

③ Use two pairs of **inverted commas** to punctuate this sentence.

Stop! screamed the man. You're

about to sit on a wasp!

1 mark

---

④ What is wrong with the punctuation in this sentence?

William laughed, "I wish I could go to school every day"!

_____

_____

_____

1 mark

⑤ Which sentence has the correct punctuation?

Tick one

Serena gasped, "I need a glass of water!"	☐
Serena gasped, "I need a glass of water"!	☐
Serena gasped "I need a glass of water!"	☐
Serena gasped "I need a glass of water."	☐

1 mark

---

⑥ Add **inverted commas** to these sentences.

a. Wow, thank you for my present! said Jane.

b. Mrs Waters said, Sit down, please, everyone. It's time for maths.

c. This is my favourite book, Steve said. It's about wizards and magic!

d. I fell out of the tree and broke my arm, Jaime explained.

1 mark

Answers on page 47

Apostrophes

There are two types of apostrophe: apostrophes for contraction and possessive apostrophes.

Apostrophes for contraction

A contraction is where a word or group of words is shortened by removing some letters.
An apostrophe is used to show where letters from the original words have been missed out.

For example:

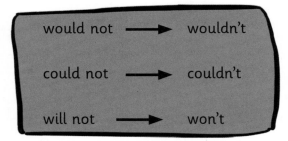

would not →	wouldn't
could not →	couldn't
will not →	won't

Can you write these contractions?

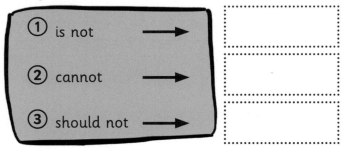

① is not →

② cannot →

③ should not →

Possessive apostrophe

Apostrophes can also be used to show possession; when a noun belongs to another noun.

For example:

The toe belongs to Isabella.

I stepped on Isabella's toe accidentally.

If the noun already ends in "s", there's no need to add another "s":

The hat belongs to James.

Sam picked up James' hat.

Always put the apostrophe after the noun – watch out for plurals!

The book belongs to the girl.   The books belongs to the girls.

I returned the girl's books.   *I returned the girls' books.*

It is a good idea to ask who the noun belongs to when working out where to put the apostrophe.

Parent Guide

When children begin to use apostrophes, they can overuse them on every plural or word that ends in "s". Don't discourage this too much as developing good judgement is an ongoing process. Ask them if something belongs to that word (to show possession). Consider unusual contractions together, e.g. shall not becomes shan't, to develop their awareness.

Practice Questions

① Edit this sentence by putting **apostrophes** in the correct places.

Peters project was amazing;

hed worked so hard.

1 mark

② Write the correct **contraction** below the underlined words.

Julia <u>has not</u> finished her homework.

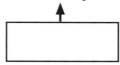

1 mark

③ How does the different position of the **apostrophes** in these sentences change their meanings?

The chick's feathers were wet.
The chicks' feathers were wet.

_____

_____

_____

1 mark

④ Circle the sentence that should contain a **possessive apostrophe**.

His bag was full of very useful things.

The dentists office was full of people.

"Is this ball yours?" the boy asked.

The ice cream van turned its music on.

1 mark

⑤ Tick the correct boxes to show which type of **apostrophe** each sentence has.

		Apostrophe for contraction	Apostrophe for possession
a.	The juggler's hands moved so fast.		
b.	I wasn't sure if I liked the ice-cream.		
c.	The wind tugged at the tree's leaves mercilessly.		
d.	She was upset as she hadn't done her homework.		

1 mark

⑥ Write these words as **contractions**.

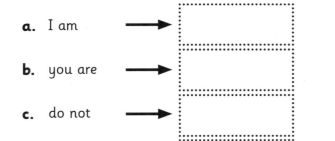

a. I am

b. you are

c. do not

d. they have

1 mark

⑦ Rewrite this sentence so that it uses the correct **apostrophes**.

Simons' bag contains lots of chocolate and hes decided to share some with his friend's.

_____

_____

_____

1 mark

Spelling

You can learn how to spell longer words by practising your word building. Words are often built with a **root word** (the main part), a **prefix** added to the start and or a **suffix** added to the end.

prefix → *illegally* ← **suffix**

↑
root
word

Choose an appropriate suffix from the box on the right to add to these words:

> Think about whether you will need to drop or change any letters at the end of the root word before adding the suffix.

Root word	+ suffix	Root word	+ suffix
judge	*judgement*	① adore	
② office		③ finance	
④ appreciate		⑤ achieve	
⑥ intent		⑦ rely	

> —ment —able
>
> —tion —cial

Add the prefix **im-** or **in-** and the suffix **–ly** to these words:

Root word	+ prefix + suffix	Root word	+ prefix + suffix
⑧ possible		⑨ visible	
⑩ patient		⑪ credible	

Spelling Challenge!

Can you think of six words that end with the suffixes **–tious** or **–cious**?

> Use a dictionary to check your spelling.

⑫ .... ⑬ .... ⑭ ....

⑮ .... ⑯ .... ⑰ ....

Practice Questions

Before you begin, look at the words in the box at the bottom of this exercise. Once you have read through them, cover the box and complete the sentences.

① _____

The man was very _____

when we explained our problem to him.

1 mark

② _____

We saw an unusual _____

running in the woods.

1 mark

③ _____

I tried to hide my _____

when I opened the door.

1 mark

④ _____

Sally was _____

because the traffic was so slow.

1 mark

⑤ _____

I was _____ trying to solve

the puzzle!

1 mark

⑥ _____

The sound was _____

a car's brakes screeching.

1 mark

⑦ _____

The newsreader warned of an

_____ disease that we

should protect ourselves against.

1 mark

⑧ _____

It was a _____ day and we

wanted to celebrate as a family.

1 mark

reasonable	special	actually	worried
infectious	creature	reaction	clueless

More Spellings

Silent Letters

Some spellings are tricky because they have letters that you cannot hear when you say the word.

① Circle the silent letters in each of these words:

a. m u s c l e   **b.** t h u m b   **c.** c h o r u s   **d.** h o n e s t   **e.** a n s w e r   **f.** i s l a n d

Look at those words closely for one minute and then cover them up. Write the correct spelling next to each definition:

② .... telling the truth

③ .... a strong body part

④ .... one on each hand

⑤ .... a musical part

⑥ .... place for shipwreck

⑦ .... reply to someone

The letter string "ough"

Words with the letter string "**ough**" are particularly difficult to spell because it can make so many different sounds!

⑧

Find eight words that contain 'ough' in the wordsearch and write them in these boxes.

N	J	E	N	O	U	G	H	F	V
Y	Y	M	D	O	Q	B	S	G	T
R	O	U	G	H	P	U	T	G	I
T	H	O	R	O	U	G	H	E	H
O	C	T	T	O	D	B	R	G	P
U	O	A	F	H	O	D	O	S	L
G	U	E	M	U	W	O	U	B	O
H	G	K	G	K	N	F	G	G	U
W	H	Z	J	E	U	P	H	M	G
G	I	N	B	O	U	G	H	B	H

Homophones

Homophones are words that sound the same but are spelt differently and have different meaning. Can you think of five different homophones?

sale / sail

⑨

⑩

⑪

⑫

⑬

Answers on page 48

Practice Questions

Before you begin, look at the words in the box at the bottom of this page. Once you have read through them, cover the box and complete these sentences.

①

I was careful not to drop a

_____ from the table.

1 mark

②

My sister _____ down the

last step and fell into a bush.

1 mark

③

Ted thought it was a _____

spelling test.

1 mark

④

The hairdresser made sure that she cleaned her

_____ carefully.

1 mark

⑤

It was fascinating to listen to the local

_____ about the wishing well.

1 mark

⑥

The museum curator spoke

_____ about the box.

1 mark

⑦

The knight thrust his _____

towards the onrushing dragon.

1 mark

⑧

I walked across the sweltering

_____ for many days.

1 mark

| crumb | tumbled | scissors | myth |
| tough | desert | sword | insightfully |

Reading: Retrieving Information

Finding information in a text is a really important skill. You have to skim the words to find what you're looking for. Don't be tempted to THINK that you know the answer!

> **You must FIND IT, PROVE IT.**

This means that you look for words that relate to the question you have to answer, underline them, read the sentence again and prove to yourself that this is the right information for the question.

Read the information on the opposite page about The Solar System and answer the questions.

① How many Earths could fit inside the Sun?

1 mark

② What keeps the planets on their path around the Sun?

1 mark

③ Name two dwarf planets.

1 mark

④ Which section would inform a reader about forces in space?

Write the name of the subheading.

1 mark

⑤ Find and copy a piece of evidence from the text to support these two statements.

	Statement	Evidence
a.	There is an unusual aroma on Venus.	
b.	Comets are large.	

1 mark

Answers on page 48

The Solar System is the part of space that's home to our local star (the Sun) and everything that travels around it. This includes eight planets, five dwarf planets, more than 170 moons and countless other bits of ice and rock.

THE SUN

The Sun is a huge ball of hot gas, far bigger than anything else in the Solar System. Over a million Earths could fit inside. It's incredibly hot and bright, giving off heat and light that shines across the whole Solar System. At its surface, the Sun is hot enough to boil diamonds and at its centre, it reaches an unimaginable 15 million °C (15,000,000 °C), fired by burning, churning nuclear reactions in its core.

THE PLANETS

Planets are huge balls of rock or gas that orbit (travel around) a star. Eight planets orbit our Sun. The four closest are the rocky planets. They have hard, rocky surfaces with hot molten rock and metal underneath. The other four are the gas giants, huge globes of swirling gases and icy liquids.

- Mercury is the closest planet to the Sun and the smallest planet in the entire Solar System. The temperature on Mercury swings from a scorching 430°C in the day to a freezing −180°C at night.
- Venus is wrapped in a thick atmosphere (blanket of gas), making it the hottest planet in the Solar System. Venus' atmosphere also has swirling clouds of acid that smell like rotten eggs and can burn through metal.
- Earth is the third planet from the Sun, and the only planet known to support life. It is the only planet in our Solar System to have oceans of liquid water on its surface.
- Mars is a small, dry, cold planet. It's sometimes called the "Red Planet" because its soil is a rusty red colour. Robots called rovers explore Mars' surface, doing experiments and sending photos to scientists on Earth.

The planets are kept on their curving paths around the Sun by a force called gravity. This is the force that pulls things together. The heavier something is, the more gravity it has. Without the pull of the Sun's gravity, all the planets would fly off into outer space.

ASTEROIDS, COMETS AND DWARF PLANETS

As well as the eight planets, the Solar System is also home to lots of smaller bits of rock and ice.

- Asteroids are chunks of rock, ranging in size from grains of sand to massive boulders.
- Comets are balls of ice and dust, the size of a small town. They orbit the Sun in wide ovals, trailing icy tails behind them.
- Dwarf planets, like Pluto and Ceres, orbit the Sun and are smaller than true planets.

Parent Guide

Skim reading and fact retrieval are important skills children must practise. Encourage them to "**find it, prove it**" for each question: look back at the information and underline the sentence that relates. Then they should use these words to form the basis of their answer.

Reading: Inference

Another important reading skill is to understand what is happening in a story, for example, *how* people are feeling or *why* they are behaving a certain way. The author might not state this clearly but may give **clues** that you will need to find and understand. This is called **inference**. It is important to use words from the text as clues to prove your answer.

Read the Norse tale on the opposite page and answer the questions.

① **Why** did Thrym *chuckle* when he saw Loki?

_____

_____

_____

1 mark

② **Why** were Thor's eyes *flashing* with anger through the veil?

_____

_____

_____

1 mark

③ Find one piece of evidence to support the following statement:

Loki enjoyed the day's events.

_____

_____

_____

1 mark

④ Thrym was surprised a number of times by his "bride". Name two things that **surprised** him:

_____

_____

_____

1 mark

⑤ Complete the table by ticking **true or false** for each statement.

	Statement	True	False
a.	Freya was happy to follow any plan.		
b.	Thrym lived in the land of the gods.		
c.	Thor was hesitant about Loki's plan.		

1 mark

Parent Guide

Inference skills can be developed from a young age by discussing stories with your child. Look at the pictures together and talk about them. Ask questions about the text to help your child to analyse why things are happening or how people are feeling, helping them to find evidence to support their ideas.

THOR'S WEDDING - A TALE FROM NORSE MYTHOLOGY

Thor the thunder god had a hammer that was so powerful it could flatten a mountain. He slept with it beside his bed, but one morning he woke up to find it had disappeared. He called for Loki, the trickster god, who was the most cunning person he knew.

"Your hammer is our main weapon against the giants," mused Loki. "I bet the giants have stolen it."

Loki borrowed a magical feathered cloak from the goddess Freya. The cloak whirled him through the sky to the land of giants. He found Thrym, the giant king, sitting on a hill with the top of his head in the clouds. Thrym chuckled when he saw Loki.

"I know what you are looking for," he said, "but I will not return Thor's hammer until Freya is my wife."

Loki winged his way back to the land of the gods and told Thor the news. The thunder god called for Freya at once and commanded her to go to the land of the giants.

"Put on a veil and a wedding dress," he said. "Today you will marry Thrym, the giant king."

"I will NOT!" Freya said, scornfully. "You can marry him if you like him so much."

"Don't be angry with Freya," Loki said to Thor, hiding a smile. "It's a great idea! You can dress as a bride, and I will dress as a bridesmaid, and we will trick Thrym into handing you back your hammer."

Grumbling under his breath, Thor changed into a sparkling dress and covered his face with a veil. Loki did the same, then they set off for the land of the giants. Thrym had prepared a wedding feast and sent for a priest to conduct the ceremony. He took Thor by the hand and they sat down together.

"You can choose whatever food you would like, Freya, my love," he said. So, Thor ate a whole ox and fifty bowls of beans, and washed it down with three barrels of mead. Thrym was astonished. "What an appetite she has!" he gasped.

"I am sure she is just nervous about her wedding day," said Loki the bridesmaid, soothingly.

"How sweet!" said Thrym. He tried to glimpse his bride's face through the veil, but could only see Thor's eyes, flashing with anger. "What fearsome eyes she has!"

"I am sure she is just excited about her wedding day," said Loki, calmly.

"I am, too," said Thrym. He tried to lift up the veil to kiss his bride, but Thor backed away.

"I am sure she will let you kiss her after you are married," said Loki, hurriedly.

"Then let us wait no longer!" declared Thrym. "Bring the mighty hammer of Thor and lay it on my beautiful bride's lap so that the priest can bless our wedding."

As soon as the hammer was on his lap, Thor grasped it in both hands and swung it around his head, knocking Thrym to the ground. He tore off his veil and stomped away, smashing things with his hammer.

"Poor Thrym will be very disappointed," said Loki, as they made their way back to the land of the gods. "After all, you did make a very beautiful bride!"

Reading: Vocabulary

The last important reading skill is to understand what each word means. When you are reading, it is a good idea to look up new words in a dictionary to find out their meaning, or ask an adult. You can also use the text to help you work out the meaning of a word. Read the sentence again. Think of a word that you could replace the new word with so that the sentence still makes sense.

Read the extract from Alice in Wonderland on the opposite page and answer the questions.

① *"You may nurse it for a bit, if you like!" the Duchess said to Alice, flinging the baby at her as she spoke.*

This sentence suggests that the Duchess was which one of the following?

Tick one

Heartfelt

Nurturing

Reckless

Compassionate

1 mark

② What does the word **low** mean in the sentence?

Then they both bowed low and their curls got entangled.

_____

_____

_____

_____

_____

1 mark

③ Find and copy **one word from the first paragraph** which shows what the footman did when he reached the door.

1 mark

④ Find and copy **one word from the third paragraph** which suggests that Alice is a hesitant character.

1 mark

⑤ Find and copy **one word from the fourth paragraph** which shows that the howling and sneezing did not stop.

1 mark

Answers on page 48

For a minute or two she stood looking at the house, when suddenly a footman came running out of the wood (judging by his face only, she would have called him a fish) and rapped loudly at the door with his knuckles. It was opened by another footman, with a round face and large eyes like a frog.

The Fish-Footman began by producing from under his arm a great letter, and he handed it over to the other, saying, in a solemn tone, "For the Duchess. An invitation from the Queen to play croquet." The Frog-Footman repeated, in the same solemn tone, "From the Queen. An invitation for the Duchess to play croquet." Then they both bowed low and their curls got entangled together.

When Alice next peeped out, the Fish-Footman was gone, and the other was sitting on the ground near the door, staring stupidly up into the sky. Alice went timidly up to the door and knocked.

"There's no sort of use in knocking," said the Footman, "for two reasons. First, because I'm on the same side of the door as you; secondly, because they're making such a noise inside, no one could possibly hear you." And certainly there was a most extraordinary noise going on within – a constant howling and sneezing, and every now and then a great crash, as if a dish or kettle had been broken to pieces.

"How am I to get in?" asked Alice.

Alice opened the door and went in. The door led right into a large kitchen, which was full of smoke from one end to the other; the Duchess was sitting on a three-legged stool in the middle, nursing a baby; the cook was leaning over the fire, stirring a large cauldron which seemed to be full of soup.

"There's certainly too much pepper in that soup!" Alice said to herself, as well as she could for sneezing. Even the Duchess sneezed occasionally; and as for the baby, it was sneezing and howling alternately without a moment's pause. The only two creatures in the kitchen that did not sneeze were the cook and a large cat, which was grinning from ear to ear.

"Please would you tell me," said Alice, a little timidly, "why your cat grins like that?"

"It's a Cheshire-Cat," said the Duchess, "and that's why."

"I didn't know that Cheshire-Cats always grinned; in fact, I didn't know that cats could grin," said Alice.

"You don't know much," said the Duchess, "and that's a fact."

Just then the cook took the cauldron of soup off the fire, and at once set to work throwing everything within her reach at the Duchess — the fire-irons came first; then followed a shower of saucepans, plates and dishes. The Duchess took no notice of them, even when they hit her.

"Oh, please mind what you're doing!" cried Alice, jumping up and down in an agony of terror.

"Here! You may nurse it a bit, if you like!" the Duchess said to Alice, flinging the baby at her as she spoke. "I must go and get ready to play croquet with the Queen," and she hurried out of the room.

Parent Guide

Vocabulary is not built purely by reading or hearing words. Encourage your child to become an "active reader" – engaging with the story and asking the meaning of words. Demonstrate enthusiasm whenever you hear new words by looking them up together and discussing synonyms.

Answers

Page 4 – Nouns and Adjectives

1 Common nouns: **classroom, plant, bucket, gnome**
Proper nouns: **Mrs Smith, England, Jennifer**
2 **it**
Various answers are possible – examples:

3	**she**	**6**	**tall**
4	**our**	**7**	**red**
5	**delicious**	**8**	**deep**

Page 5 – Nouns and Adjectives Practice Questions

1 **A pronoun**
2 **magnificent, red, orange**
3 **Amelie, teddy, happiness**
4 **L**aura, **E**dinburgh, **J**ohn, **T**uesday
5 **George swatted at the <u>fly</u> wearily.**
6 *Various answers are possible – example:* **excitement**
7 **she** and **her**
8 friend**ly**

Page 6 – Verbs and Adverbs

1	**was, slept**	**5**	**quickly** and **twice**
2	**thought, told**	**6**	**should**
3	**carefully**	**7**	**might**
4	**merrily**		

Page 7 – Verbs and Adverbs Practice Questions

1 **was, tested, recommended** and **wear**
2a **Adverb**
2b **Adjective**
3 *Various answers are possible – examples:* **Changes the activity to a possibility, rather than a definite.**
4 **I <u>hastily</u> unwrapped the present.**
5 **happily**
6 **early**
7 **would**
8 **laughed**

Page 8 – Determiners and Prepositions

1 Articles: **the**
Determiners: **many, some** and **two**
2 Articles: **A, the** and **an**
3 **during** and **up**
4 **through** and **before**
5 **behind** and **by**

Page 9 – Determiners and Prepositions Practice Questions

1 **a, any** and **the**
2 **During, on** and **under**
3 **Article**
4 **a tambourine, some bananas, an octopus**
5 *Various answers are possible – examples:* **down, through**
6 **an** or **the**
7 Determiners: **those, every, the** and **an**
Articles: **under, between, after** and **on**
8 **the**

Page 10 – Synonyms and Antonyms

1a	**Quick** and **Rapid**	**3**	**comforting**
1b	**Amiable** and **Friendly**	**4**	**new**
1c	**Sleepy** and **Tired**	**5**	**serious**
1d	**Tall** and **Towering**	**6**	**laugh**
1e	**Unusual** and **Rare**	**7**	**weak**
1f	**Mad** and **Eccentric**	**8**	**calm**
	Various answers are possible - examples:	**9**	**boring**
2	**horrible**		

Page 11 – Synonyms and Antonyms Practice Questions

1 **Insignificant**
2 **captured** and **trapped**
3 **Endless**
4 *Various answers are possible – examples:* **horrible**
5 **Antonyms**
6 *Various answers are possible – examples:* **gross, nasty, horrid, rubbish**
7a **Precisely** and **Exactly**
7b **Joyful** and **Happy**
7c **Real** and **Authentic**
7d **Loyal** and **Devoted**
8 *Various answers are possible – examples:* **cold** and **freezing**

Page 12 – Subject and Object

1 bird
2 fireworks
3 man
4 Sarah
5 hair
6 test
7 floor
8 brush

Page 13 – Subject and Object Practice Questions

1a subject
1b object
1c subject
1d object
2a object
2b subject
2c subject
2d object
3 tree
4 Subject: **children** and **they**
 Objects: **stairs** and **football**

5a subject
5b object
6 She, them
7a subject
7b object
8a subject
8b verb
8c adjective
8d object

Page 14 – Clauses

1a main clause
1b subordinate clause
2a subordinate clause
2b main clause
3 that was delicious
4 whose ball had bounced over the fence.
5 that had bunk beds inside.
6 who is now hiding under the car

Page 15 – Clauses Practice Questions

1 subordinate clause
2 *Various answers are possible – examples:*
 which had gone mouldy
3 main clause
4 that looked appealing and whose
 nose fell off
5a subordinate clause
5b subordinate clause
5c main clause
5d main clause
6 While Bailey slept on the sofa
7 because he had always wanted a cat

Page 16 – Phrases

1 a new watch
2 The rickety roller-coaster
3 The boy with the stripy trainers
4 The purple house
5 Last night, I played football.
6 Under the bridge, we chatted.
7 *Various answers are possible – example:*
 At the bus stop,

Page 17 – Phrases Practice Questions

1 Noun phrase
2 Last Tuesday
3 the tall, strong tree with thick branches
4 Fronted Adverbial
5 After dinner, John painted the fence.
6 The magician had disappeared in an instant.
 Various answers are possible – example:
7 the immense, wooden wardrobe

Page 18 – Conjunctions

Various answers are possible - example:
1 but
2 Although
3 until
4 If
5 because
6 so that

Page 19 – Conjunctions Practice Questions

1 A coordinating conjunction
2 *Various answers are possible – example:*
 Changes the activity to a possibility, rather than a definite.
3 nor
4 *Various answers are possible – example:*
 Before
5 *Various answers are possible – example:*
 though
6 and
7 and, but and so

Page 20 - Tenses

1 I threw a ball to my friend, Jack.
2 I **will throw** a ball to my friend, Jack.
3 I **am** paint**ing** a picture.
4 He **is** kick**ing** a football.
5 They **are** walk**ing** around the lake.

Page 21 - Tenses Practice Questions

1 I reached up and took the toy down.
2 Sally **baked** cookies and **ate** them within five days.
3 I enjoyed an adventure book recently.
4 I am watching an amazing film.
5 I am eight years old and I have my own rabbit.
6 bought, rode, slept, worried and **found**

Page 22 - Active and Passive Voice

1	The man	6	The man
2	The candle	7	The candle
3	Stewart	8	Stewart
4	I	9	The obstacle course
5	We	10	the movie

Page 23 - Active and Passive Voice Practice Questions

1 Active voice: **a, d, e** and **h.**
  Passive voice: **b, c, f** and **g.**
2 *Various answers are possible – example:*
  The rabbit ate the lettuce.
3 *Various answers are possible – example:*
  The cake was baked by Jacqueline.
4 **The balloons were very kindly donated.**
5 *Various answers are possible – example:*
  The dog dug in the garden.

Page 24 - Standard English

1 am
2 are
3 is
4 are

5 **Hey bud! You up** for going to the park later? It **isn't** supposed to be raining. **Where'd** be a good place to meet?

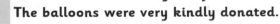

Page 25 - Standard English Practice Questions

1 I did not enjoy the film.
2 complain, was not, poor and **have**
3 They were singing beautifully.
4 I can't wait to see a dolphin.
5 bought, did and The
6 That man found my cat.
7 taught

8a	drove	8d	drank
8b	kicked	8e	found
8c	ate	8f	ran

Page 26 - Basic Punctuation

1 Can you help**?** A black dog has gone missing from the area**.** He was last seen yesterday morning. **H**e has a white tail**,** blue eyes and a red collar. Please knock at 7 King Street if you find him**.**

Page 27 - Basic Punctuation Practice Questions

1 **Are you going to bed early?**
2 As fast as possible**,** the boy ran home.
3 **What an amazing show!**
4 **Amazingly,** he escaped without blood, sweat or tears.
5a Are you playing tomorrow**?**
5b What a fantastic night**!**
5c I am very tired**.**
6 We decided that we should meet at the park and play at three o'clock. We jumped on our bikes and cycled as fast as we could towards the park. I wanted to be the first one on the swings so I pedalled really, really fast. I was like lightning!

Page 28 - More Punctuation

1 **Colon**
2 **Semi-colon**
3 **Semi-colon**
4 **Colon**

Page 29 - More Punctuation Practice Questions

1 My uncle was saving up to buy a new motorbike; he said he would take me out on it.
2 It is Rachel's goal to climb many mountains (such as Snowdon and Ben Nevis) before she is 25.
3 **I am visiting the seaside – my favourite place – next week!**
4 It is a well-presented project.
5 Laura loved holidays for two reasons: spending time with her family and getting lots of sleep!
6 The cat, who had been watching the bird all morning, finally pounced… and missed!

Page 30 - Inverted Commas

1 I replied **B**onjour!
2 I replied **"**Bonjour!**"**
3 I replied**,** "Bonjour!"
4 **"Are you having a good day?" asked John.**

Page 31 - Inverted Commas Practice Questions

1 **"Which drink would you like?" asked the waiter.**
2 **"I would love to," said Jo.**
3 **"Stop!" screamed the man. "You're about to sit on a wasp!"**
4 **The exclamation mark is outside of the inverted commas – it should be inside.**
5 **Serena gasped, "I need a glass of water!"**
6a "Wow, thank you for my present!" said Jane.
6b Mrs Waters said, "Sit down, please, everyone. It's time for maths."
6c "This is my favourite book," Steve said. "It's about wizards and magic!"
6d "I fell out of the tree and broke my arm," Jaime explained.

Page 32 - Apostrophes

1 **isn't**
2 **can't**
3 **shouldn't**

Page 33 - Apostrophes Practice Questions

1 Peter's project was amazing – he'd work so hard.
2 **hasn't**
Various answers are possible – example:
3 **By moving the apostrophe, it changes the amount of chicks from one to multiple.**
4 **The dentist's office was full of people.**
5a **Possession**
5b **Contraction**
5c **Possession**
5d **Contraction**
6a **I'm**
6b **you're**
6c **don't**
6d **they've**
7 Simon's bag contains lots of chocolate and he's decided to share some with his friends.

Page 34 - Spelling

1 ador**able** or ador**ation**
2 offi**cial**
3 finan**cial**
4 apprecia**tion** or appreci**able**
5 achieve**ment** or achieva**ble**
6 inten**tion**
7 reli**able**
8 **im**possi**bly**
9 **in**visi**bly**
10 **im**patient**ly**
11 **in**credi**bly**
Various answers are possible – examples:
12 **cautious**
13 **unconscious**
14 **nutritious**
15 **delicious**
16 **ambitious**
17 **suspicious**

Page 35 - Spelling Practice Questions

1 **reasonable**
2 **creature**
3 **reaction**
4 **worried**
5 **clueless**
6 **actually**
7 **infectious**
8 **special**

Page 36 - More Spellings

1a muscle	**2** honest
1b thum**b**	**3** muscle
1c **ch**orus	**4** thumb
1d **h**onest	**5** chorus
1e ans**w**er	**6** island
1f is**l**and	**7** answer

8

N	J	E	N	O	U	G	H	F	V
Y	Y	M	D	O	Q	B	S	G	T
R	O	U	G	H	P	U	T	G	I
T	H	O	R	O	U	G	H	E	H
O	C	T	T	O	D	B	R	G	P
U	O	A	F	H	O	D	O	S	L
G	U	E	M	U	W	O	U	B	O
H	G	K	G	K	N	F	G	G	U
W	H	Z	J	E	U	P	H	M	G
G	I	N	B	O	U	G	H	B	H

Various answers are possible — examples:

9	male/mail	**12**	pair/pear
10	won/one	**13**	see/sea
11	night/knight		

Page 37 - More Spellings Practice Questions

1	crumb	**5**	myth
2	tumbled	**6**	insightfully
3	tough	**7**	sword
4	scissors	**8**	desert

Pages 38-39 - Reading: Retrieving Information

1 Over a million
2 Gravity
3 Pluto and Ceres
4 The Planets
5a "acid that smell like rotten eggs"
5b "the size of a small town"

Pages 40-41 - Reading: Inference

Various answers are possible — examples:
1 Because he knew what Loki wanted.
2 Because he was angry that Thrym had his hammer.
3 Acceptable answers:
- Loki was "hiding a smile"
- Loki joked at the end: "After all, you did make a very beautiful bride!"

4 Acceptable answers:
- Her appetite
- Her fearsome eyes
- Why she had backed away when he tried to kiss her.

5a False
5b False
5c True

Pages 42-43 - Reading: Vocabulary

1 Reckless
Various answers are possible — examples:
2 They were close to the ground when they bowed.
3 "rapped"
4 "timidly" or "peeped"
5 "constant"